GW01466210

Weird and Wonderful

Bible stories retold by
Michael Forster

Kevin
Mayhew

First published in 1997 by
KEVIN MAYHEW LTD
Rattlesden
Bury St Edmunds
Suffolk IP30 0SZ

The stories in this book are extracted from *A story, a hug
and a prayer* (© 1994 Kevin Mayhew Ltd) and *Good night,
God bless* (© 1995 Kevin Mayhew Ltd).

0 1 2 3 4 5 6 7 8 9

ISBN 1 84003 042 9
Catalogue No 1500129

Cover by Eddy Mooney
Typesetting by Louise Hill
Printed and bound in Great Britain

SNAKE IN THE GRASS

Cecil the serpent was hiding in some bushes, thinking what a lot of fun he was going to have getting his own back. When God had made the garden, Cecil had thought he was going to be put in charge of it. Then imagine his horror when God created a completely new kind of animal and put *them* in charge. Human beings, they were called. Well, that was a silly name for an animal to begin with, and they were such newcomers! Actually, Cecil hadn't been there all that long either, as it was a new garden, but because he had been there just that bit longer he thought that made him better. 'These new animals!' he thought. 'They come in here and think they own the place!' Then he overheard God talking to the humans.

'Now,' said God, 'you can eat any fruit you find in the garden, except the fruit on that tree in the middle.'

'Why?' asked the female human, who was called Eve.

'It's the tree of knowledge,' said God, 'the knowledge of right and wrong, and you must not eat from it or you will die.'

Cecil waited a few minutes and squirmed up close to Eve.

'Ooh!' yelled Eve. 'You didn't half frighten me. What do you think you're doing, sneaking up on people like that?'

'Oh,' thought Cecil, 'it's "people" now, is it? Only here five minutes and she thinks she's a whole species.' But he put on his nicest smile and said, 'I'm ssso ssssorry to have ssscared you. I'm Sssesssil the ssserpent, and I wanted to sssay welcome to thisss Garden of Eden.'

'Well, that's very kind of you, I'm sure,' said Eve. 'No offence meant.'

'None taken,' said Cecil. 'Have you sssampled sssome of the delicasssiesss around here? Sssome of the fruit is sssimply ssscrumptiousss – essspecially that tree in the sssentre of the garden.'

'Oh,' said Eve, 'God said we mustn't eat from it or we'll die.'

'Why,' said Cecil, 'that'sss sssilly! Sssmall-minded sssensssorship! God doesssn't want you to be wise like him, that'sss all.'

Eve was interested. 'You mean,' she asked, 'that if I eat that, I'll be as wise as God?'

'Sssertain as sssunshine in Ssseptember!' answered Cecil. 'Try it – itsss sssensssational!'

Well, the fruit looked tempting – round, plump, and probably juicy, and Eve thought that to be as wise as God would be wonderful. So she took the fruit and ate it. Just then her husband Adam came along and really blew his top. 'You haven't eaten that, have you?' he said.

'Of course I have,' said Eve. 'I knew God was only trying to frighten us – here, have some.' Adam hesitated a moment, and then took the fruit and bit into it. It certainly was lovely. Just as he was enjoying it, Eve shrieked at him so that he nearly swallowed the pips.

'You haven't got any clothes on!'

'What!' exclaimed Adam, and got very embarrassed. Then he looked at Eve and said, 'Neither have you.'

Now the silly thing is they'd never had any clothes on, but they just hadn't bothered about it until they ate the fruit. But now, for some strange reason, they were rushing round the garden trying to find leaves to cover themselves with. Cecil hadn't had such a good time since he was created. He just laughed and laughed until his sides hurt – and he hadn't got any hands to hold them with!

Then he heard the sound of God's voice: 'Adam, where are you?' Adam and Eve were nowhere to be found, but were hiding from God because they were embarrassed. Eventually,

God found them and asked, 'What's going on? have you eaten from that tree?'

'It's not my fault,' babbled Adam. 'The woman made me do it.'

'Oh, that's right,' said God, 'blame the woman for it. After all, you might as well start as you mean to go on!'

Then Eve said, 'Don't blame me – Cecil made me do it!'

'What?' said God, 'Cecil the Serpent? But you're supposed to be better and more intelligent than he is.'

'Huh!' thought Cecil. 'That shows what *you* know!'

'Well,' said God, 'that's torn it! I hoped you'd all work together – people, animals, everything – but you're quarrelling and blaming one another right at the start. Life's obviously going to be difficult, and painful, and people and animals will be fighting one another, all because you couldn't just live together the way I wanted. Well, you can get out of this garden, for a start. Go and work for your livings. And as for you,' he said to Cecil, 'since you seem to enjoy saying s's, I'll fix it so that that's all you *do* say from now on.'

'Sssssssssss!' said Cecil – partly because he was angry, and partly because he couldn't say anything else. He was so embarrassed that he just lay down on his stomach and crawled away. And that's how he has been ever since. Men, women and animals carry on fighting and blaming one another, and no one ever wants to admit being wrong.

No wonder we make ourselves unhappy!

Based on Genesis 3

Rabbles and Babbles

A long, long time ago, in a land called Shinar, some people had what they thought was a great idea. They were convinced that nothing was impossible for them. They believed that all they had to do was work together, and they could do anything. Now at that time, everybody spoke the same language, so working together should have been fairly easy. 'Why,' said Barnaby (who was a nice person but not as bright as he thought he was) 'with our combined knowledge and skills, we could climb right up to heaven!'

Barnaby's friend, Johnny, wasn't so sure. 'To begin with,' he said, 'how do you know exactly where heaven is? Things might be a lot more complicated than you think.'

'Oh, don't be stupid!' scoffed Barnaby. 'Heaven's got to be up there; it's not down here, so that's the only place left. And where do you think all that light comes from?'

'I know it looks that easy,' said Johnny, 'but things might not be quite as they seem.'

Barnaby was impatient, and might have called Johnny a name like 'philosopher', but it hadn't been invented. So he just said, 'Look, it's very simple. What you see is what there is. Don't make things complicated by asking unnecessary questions. This is earth, and heaven's up there. That's how it looks, and that's how it is.'

Johnny didn't like arguing with Barnaby, because he always felt so inferior; Barnaby seemed to know so much, and to be so confident, and Johnny always ended up feeling silly. Still, he couldn't resist saying, 'Perhaps God doesn't want us to climb up to heaven – if that's where it is. Perhaps that's why we can't see it.'

Barnaby thought this was the silliest idea Johnny had had so far. 'Of course God wants us to do it!' he said, scornfully. 'Would he have made us so wonderfully clever, and taught us how to build towers and things if he didn't want us to do it?'

Johnny opened his mouth to ask another question, but Barnaby held up his hand. 'No more!' he said. 'We have a duty to use all the knowledge we have. That's what God expects. So whatever we're capable of doing must be right.'

Johnny thought, 'I'm capable of punching you on the nose, but it wouldn't be right to do it!' But he didn't say that, because he knew Barnaby would have an answer. Barnaby always did!

So everyone set to work – everyone except Johnny and Barnaby, that is. Johnny didn't join in because he thought it was wrong, and Barnaby didn't do any work because he thought he was too important. 'I'm an ideas man,' he used to say. 'I must save my creative energy, and let less important people do the actual work.'

Surprisingly, most of the other people joined in. They were deeply impressed by Barnaby's confidence, and thought Johnny was a very silly man. So the diggers dug the foundations, and the stone masons got the stones ready and started building while the carpenters put in the beams to support the wooden staircase. They were really excited about getting to heaven, and they worked terribly hard every day.

God wasn't happy about it, though. He hadn't
put people on earth so that they could spend
all their time trying to get back to heaven! He
could see what was really happening, and he
didn't like it. The people who were building
the tower were so obsessed with it that they

forgot about everything else. They never played with their children, or looked after their elderly relations. They started to think that the tower was all that mattered; so anybody who wasn't strong enough to work on it was ignored. A lot of people were unhappy, because they weren't wanted, and of course if anyone was ill, and couldn't work, nobody had time to look after them. Some people even died from neglect. All the workers were interested in doing was trying to get to heaven! So God got very angry. 'I'm going to teach them a lesson,' he thought, 'and give them something else to think about.'

So it was that, one morning, Barnaby got up and went out as usual to find an unpleasant surprise awaiting him. He'd have known about it earlier if he'd listened to his wife that morning, but he never did that – he just used to get up and rush straight out to see how the tower was getting on. This particular morning, as he got near to the tower, he heard the most amazing sound – a loud babbling of lots of people all shouting at one another at the tops of their voices. So Barnaby went up and tried to silence them, but he had to get a whistle and blow it before they noticed him. When they did, he started telling them off.

'You're supposed to be building this tower,' he shouted at them, 'not gossiping amongst yourselves – now get on with it!'

Barnaby couldn't understand why the people were looking at him in such a strange, bewildered way. Then the foreman came up and spoke to him, and it was Barnaby's turn to look amazed. He couldn't understand anything the foreman was saying. 'What's the matter with you?' he yelled at the foreman. 'Talk properly so that I can understand you.'

The foreman couldn't understand a word Barnaby was saying, and realised that Barnaby couldn't understand him, either, but he thought it was all Barnaby's fault. Barnaby seemed to be making some very strange noises indeed. So the foreman tried again – but louder. Barnaby still couldn't understand and he shouted back – louder still. Then all the others joined in, and before long everyone was shouting at everyone else, and nobody was listening – even if they had been able to understand!

You know what had happened, don't you? They were all speaking different languages! Everything everybody said made sense – but only to them! No one could understand anybody else at all!

So the tower never got finished.

And it won't be. God is still trying to teach us that heaven isn't in the sky; the way to find heaven is to care about other people, and learn to understand each other.

And all this time later, we're still not very good at it!

Based on Genesis 11:1-9

HAVING A WHALE OF A TIME

Jonah was a fairly ordinary sort of chap really, rather like people we know, except that he lived a very long time ago, and a very long way away from here, in Israel. He enjoyed looking after his garden, and chatting with his neighbours but, like many other people then and now, there was something about him that really was not very nice. And we'll see what that was in a minute.

Jonah had often thought that he'd like to do something really special for God, and he used to day-dream about the brave things he might do – rescuing people from torture, or saving someone who was drowning, or perhaps stopping a robbery. Other times, he would dream about becoming a doctor, or a great lawyer . . .

But God had a different idea. That's the thing about God – just when we think we've worked out what we'd like to do for him, he thinks of something different! So he told Jonah to go to Nineveh, a very large town, and give them a message. The people in Nineveh were living very badly. They were lying, they were stealing, they were fighting with one another – in fact Nineveh was not a good place to be at all. So the message Jonah had to give them was that they had to change and start being good to one another, because if they went on like that, they would all end up being killed.

You might expect Jonah to be pleased that God had such an important job for him – but he wasn't. As I told you, Jonah was really quite an ordinary, and rather nice person, but he had one very bad point indeed. 'Why should I go to Nineveh?' he thought. 'It's not in this country. All the people there are foreigners – why should I help them?'

That was Jonah's bad point – he thought that anybody who was from another country was bad, and he only wanted to help his own people. 'After all,' he thought, 'there are plenty of people here who lie and steal and fight. I should really go to them, not to some foreign place. When all's said and done, charity begins at home!' But he knew it was no good arguing with God, who had quite made up his mind that Jonah was to go to Nineveh.

The more Jonah thought about it, the less he wanted to go. 'I know,' he thought, 'I'll run away to Spain, and hide from God.' So he went down to the docks at a place called Joppa, and said to the man in the ticket office, 'I'd like to go to Spain, please.' The man took Jonah's money, handed him a ticket and pointed to a ship. 'There you are,' he said, 'take the third ship along.'

Jonah boarded the ship and settled down for a long cruise, wondering whether God had noticed yet, that he'd run away. Poor old Jonah didn't understand that you can't run away from God – but he was about to find out! They hadn't been at sea very long when the most horrible storm began. The wind and waves were throwing the little ship about on the sea, while the thunder and lightning was frightening everyone, even the really tough sailors! They were all wondering what they ought to do, and Jonah was getting more and more frightened because he knew!

After a little while, he did a very brave thing. He went to the captain and said, 'It's all my fault. I'm running away from God, and as long as I'm here, this storm's going to go on. I-I-I think you'd better th-th-throw me overboard.'

'Good grief!' said the captain, 'We can't do that! What would your God do to us if we did a thing like that?' But the storm got even worse, and the sailors got even more frightened, and eventually they decided to do what Jonah said. So over the side he went, with all the sailors praying like mad, asking God not to be angry! As soon as Jonah hit the water, the storm stopped. All the sailors were very pleased – but what about Jonah?

God hadn't forgotten Jonah, and he sent a very big fish, which opened its mouth and swallowed Jonah whole – which was a good thing, really! Imagine Jonah's surprise, when he looked around! 'Well!' he thought, 'I wonder how I get out of here.' But he couldn't think of a way that he really fancied very much, so he decided to sit and wait. Three days he was there. Can you imagine being shut up in a stuffy, smelly place for three whole days and nights? Still, it gave him a bit of time to think and, although he still didn't like the idea of being nice to 'foreigners', he realised that running away from God

was rather silly. So he decided that if he got out of there in one piece, he'd do what God wanted!

When the three days were up, God got the fish to put Jonah back onto dry land – not far from Nineveh. This time, Jonah did what God had wanted. He walked right through the city, telling everyone to change, before it was too late. And the amazing thing is that they listened to him. They stopped lying, and cheating, and fighting, and life became very good indeed.

Jonah wasn't very pleased about that, because he still didn't like the people he called 'foreigners'. But the strange thing was that the person whom that made unhappy was Jonah himself.

Isn't that a shame?

Based on the Book of Jonah

THE BARLEY AND THE BINDWEED

Sally and Jake were both farmers, and they had been friends once although they farmed in very different ways. The difference was that Jake was greedy. He always farmed every bit of his land, and never left anything behind when he harvested. He grew as much as he possibly could and he ensured that every grain of wheat, every apple and pear, every potato and cucumber was sold at the very best possible price. Every single square inch of Jake's farm was always growing something.

Sally was a lot more relaxed about things. She used to leave a bit of one of her fields wild to encourage butterflies and other beautiful wildlife. Jake thought she was mad.

'You'll never make any money out of butterflies,' he used to say. 'You have to get everything you can out of your land – that's what good farming's about.'

Sally just smiled to herself. 'Poor old Jake,' she thought. 'He'll learn the hard way.' Then she gave orders to her workers to vary the crops each year so that the fields had a change, and always to leave one field without anything growing in it. 'We've got to take care of the land,' she used to say, 'and not ask too much of it. Then it will take care of us.'

Jake thought this was just a load of sentimental nonsense. 'It's a matter of good stewardship,' he used to say. 'You've got to get all you can from the land.'

'No,' said Sally. 'Good stewardship is about caring for the land – and it'll give you more in the long run.'

'Bah! Humbug!' exclaimed Jake, and waited for Sally to go bankrupt. 'When she does, I can buy her fields at a knockdown price,' he thought. 'Then I'll show her how a *real* farmer works the land!'

Well, Jake watched and waited, and every harvest he thought he'd see Sally packing it in because it wasn't paying. But what he actually saw was Sally's farm doing better and better.

After a little while, Jake's farm started to

produce smaller crops. 'I can't understand it,' his foreman said one day. 'The cabbages always used to do well in that field, but for the last year or two they've definitely been smaller.'

'Same goes for the wheat,' said Jake, sadly. 'The crop's got smaller every year for four years now. Well, we'll just have to put more seed in to make up for it.'

Sally overheard the conversation. 'If you don't mind my saying so,' she said, 'that'll just make it worse. You're taking all the goodness out of the land. Why not give it a rest for a year, and grow something different?'

'I do mind you saying so, actually,' snapped Jake. 'You go and mind your own business, Mrs. Knowitall!'

Jake was really jealous of Sally. 'She doesn't work half as hard as I do,' he complained to his foreman. 'And just look at her crops!'

Well, the years went by and Jake just could not understand what was happening. Sally's farm was thriving, with lovely rich soil producing good crops – except for whichever field it was that was resting of course – while Jake's crops got smaller and smaller. Then his soil began to go all powdery and dry, and every time there was a strong wind some of it blew away and landed on Sally's farm. 'That's the problem!' thought Jake. 'She's got better soil than I have. It's not fair.' The more he thought about it, the more jealous he became – and he longed to find a way of spoiling Sally's farm. Then he had an idea. And what an idea it was!

Although he couldn't grow good food crops any more, Jake had plenty of thistles and dandelions, and enormous quantities of bindweed because they will grow anywhere, as any gardener will tell you. So he dug up some of them, and put them into his greenhouse.

When the weeds grew big, Jake very carefully saved all the seeds they produced, and then late at night, while Sally was fast asleep in bed, he put his plan into action. He went out, wearing his darkest clothes so that he wouldn't be seen, and headed for Sally's best fields. And there, among the wheat and barley crops, he scattered the thistle, dandelion and bindweed seeds. Then he sneaked home and waited for the crops to ripen. Every day, he would look over his hedge as Sally passed and say, 'How're the crops doing then, Sally?'

'Very nicely, thank you,' Sally used to reply, wondering why Jake was suddenly being so nice.

She was still wondering about this when, one morning, her foreman came running up and said, 'Quick! Come and look at the fields!' Sally hurried off to see what all the fuss was about, and there – all mixed in among the crops – were thousands of nasty looking weeds.

'I can't think what went wrong,' stammered the foreman apologetically.

'Don't worry, it's not your fault,' Sally assured him. 'This is sabotage, and I think I know who's done it.'

'Well, I'd better get them out,' said the foreman and started giving orders. 'Hey, you two! Get some tools, we've got weeding to do.'

'Oh no! Don't do that!' exclaimed Sally. 'You'll probably pull up some good plants as well. No, just let them grow together. My crops are strong enough to stand a bit of opposition from a few weeds. When we harvest it, that will be the time to separate them out.'

So that is exactly what they did. Sally was quite right: her crop stood up to the weeds very well, and when the harvest time came they had a grand sort out.

Jake's little plan hadn't worked at all. In fact, it was he who went out of business because he'd destroyed the very land his business depended on. Then Sally bought his farm at a bargain price and set about correcting the harm that Jake had done.

Based on Matthew 13:24-30

RAIN, RAIN, GO AWAY

Jesus decided it was time to go home. It had been a long, hard day, and he was tired. He knew his friends were tired, too. The trouble was, they had to get across to the other side of Lake Galilee. So they had quite a journey ahead of them. 'Come on,' he said to his disciples, 'let's go home.'

So they got into the boat and pushed off into the lake. Peter was a little uneasy. He knew that storms could suddenly start on that lake, and their boat was not very big. So he told the rest of the disciples to keep a good look-out.

'You go up to the front, Andrew,' said Peter, 'and Thomas, you go to the back. Keep a special watch on those clouds just over the hills – I don't like the look of them!' (I expect Peter would actually have said 'bow' and 'stern' normally, but not all the disciples were used to being in boats, so he made it easy for them.)

'Well,' said Jesus, 'I think I'll just go and lie down in the back of the boat.' And it wasn't long before he was fast asleep.

'What do those clouds look like, Thomas?' asked Peter. 'Not very good,' replied Thomas, 'they're very black, and they're coming this way.'

'Right!' said Peter, 'Philip, you and James get that sail down, or the wind will turn us right over. Judas and John, make sure all the heavy boxes are tied down, and everyone else, sit down and hang on tight!' He'd hardly got the words out before a sudden wind hit the boat and blew it out towards the middle of the lake. It whipped up the waves until they were as high as houses and the little boat was being tossed around on the top of the sea. Some of the waves came over the side, and the boat began to fill with water. Everyone was very frightened indeed. Everyone except Jesus that is, who was still fast asleep in the back. 'Well! Look at that!' said Thomas. 'We're working like mad to keep the boat afloat, and he's just lying there, sleeping!'

Peter went over to Jesus and shook him. 'Look,' he said, 'the boat's likely to sink any minute, and you're just lying there. Don't you care if we die?'

Jesus got up and went to the front of the boat. There he shouted to the wind and the sea. 'Stop it!' he said, 'Be quiet!' Peter was about to say, 'Well, a fat lot of good that will do!' when he noticed that it had gone quiet. The boat had stopped rocking and it wasn't filling with water any more. He tried to speak, but was so amazed that he just stood there, with his mouth open, looking for all the world like a fish! Jesus went over to him and put his hand on his shoulder. 'Why are you all so afraid?' he asked. 'Didn't you trust me?'

'Wh-wh-what's going on?' stammered Peter.

'Who is this man?' asked Andrew.

'I can't believe it!' said John, 'Even the wind and the sea do as he tells them!'

Jesus smiled and quietly went to sit in the back of the boat again, until they all got to the shore. 'There!' he said, 'Now we can all get some sleep!'

Based on Mark 4:35-41

Now you've finished this book, remember that there are seven others in the series to collect:

God's Funny Ways
What We Need Is Love
Women Too!
Animal Tales
Hairy Prophets
With Friends Like These
Great Escapes